PIRKEI AVOT

Ethics
of Our Ancestors

Jewish Ethical

פרקי אבות

There is no known book without mistakes. Therefore, I ask in every language of application if anyone has any questions, comments, clarifications, corrections, please send to: **simchatchaim@yahoo.com**

All material used in this section may not be used for commercial purposes, but only for study and teaching.

To get this book or books and information Email me at:

simchatchaim@yahoo.com

Copyright©All Rights Reserved to

www.simchatchaim.com

YB"S©All rights reserved to the Editor

First Edition 2023

PIRKEI Introduction AVOT

TABLE OF CONTENTS

Page	Contents
2	Introduction
5	Chapter One
11	Chapter Two
19	Chapter Three
29	Chapter Four
37	Chapter Five
49	Chapter Six

PIRKEI　Introduction　AVOT

About Ethics of Our Ancestors

Atop Mount Sinai, over the course of forty days and nights, G-d taught Moses the entire Torah. The Torah was a two-part study: the "Written Torah," transcribed in the Five Books of Moses (and later extended to include all the 24 books of the Scriptures), and the "Oral Torah," a commentary on the Written Torah. The Oral Torah was orally transmitted from teacher to student for many generations. In the 2nd century CE, Rabbi Judah the Prince felt that the Oral Law would be forgotten unless it was transcribed. So, he compiled the basics into a six-part document called the Mishnah.

Pirkei Avot, also spelled as Pirkei Avoth or Pirkei Avos or Pirke Aboth, which translates to English as Chapters of the Fathers, is a compilation of the ethical teachings and maxims from Rabbinical Jewish tradition. It is part of didactic Jewish ethical literature. Because of its contents, the name is sometimes given as Ethics of the Fathers. Pirkei Avot consists of the Mishnaic tractate of Avot, plus one additional chapter. Avot is unique in that it is the only tractate of the Mishnah dealing solely with ethical and moral principles; there is little or no halacha (laws) found in Pirkei Avot.

The Mishnaic tractate Avot consists of five chapters. It begins with an order of transmission of the Oral Tradition; Moses receives the Torah at Mount Sinai and

PIRKEI — Introduction — AVOT

then transmits it through various generations (including Joshua, the Elders, and the Neviim, but notably not the Kohanim), whence it finally arrives at the Great Assembly, i.e., the Rabbis (Avot 1:1). It contains sayings attributed to sages from Simon the Just (200 BCE) to shortly after Judah haNasi (200 CE), redactor of the Mishnah. These aphorisms concern proper ethical and social conduct, as well as the importance of Torah study.

The first two chapters proceed in a general chronological order, with the second focusing on the students of Yochanan Ben Zakkai. Chapters Three and Four are thematic and contain various attributed sayings in no explicit order. Chapter Five departs from the organization and content of the preceding four in that it consists mostly of anonymous sayings structured around numerical lists, several of which have no direct connection with ethics. The last four paragraphs of this chapter return to the format of moral aphorisms attributed to specific rabbis.

In liturgical use, and in most printed editions of Avot, a sixth chapter, Kinyan Torah ("Acquisition of Torah") is added; this is in fact the eighth (in the Vilna edition) chapter of tractate Kallah, one of the minor tractates. It is added because its content and style are somewhat similar to that of the original tractate Avot (although it focuses on Torah study more than ethics), and to allow for one chapter to be recited on each Shabbat of the Omer period, this chapter being seen well-suited to Shabbat Shavuot, when the giving of the Torah is celebrated. (See below.) The term Pirkei Avot refers to the composite six-chapter work (Avot plus Kinyan Torah).

PIRKEI — Introduction — AVOT

Modern scholars suggest that Avot 5:21 ("He would say: Age five to Bible [study], age 10 to mishna [study]...") was not authored by Rabbi Yehudah ben Teimah (the author of 5:20, and seemingly the referent of "He would say" in 5:21) but rather by Shmuel ha-Katan, and was not part of the Mishna tractate of Avot, but rather added later to Pirkei Avot. In Machzor Vitry, for example, this passage is printed after the words "Tractate Avot has ended".

"The structure of the tractate differs greatly from the thematic structure of the other tractates and Avot sayings employ a highly stylized language instead of the clear and straightforward mishnaic prose. In addition, the anomalous character of Avot is heightened by the biblical influences on its linguistic expressions, grammatical forms, and vocabulary."

Pirkei Avot is typically printed with a sixth chapter, which however was originally part of the minor tractate Kallah Rabbati and not part of the Mishnaic tractate Avot, and was added for liturgical reasons, so that a chapter could be recited on every Shabbat between Passover and Shavuot.

Chapter 1

Mishnah 1

Moses received the Torah at Sinai and transmitted it to Joshua, Joshua to the elders, and the elders to the prophets, and the prophets to the Men of the Great Assembly. They said three things: Be patient in [the administration of] justice, raise many disciples and make a fence round the Torah:

Mishnah 2

Shimon the Righteous was one of the last of the men of the great assembly. He used to say: the world stands upon three things: the Torah, the Temple service, and the practice of acts of piety:

Mishnah 3

Antigonus a man of Socho received [the oral tradition] from Shimon the Righteous. He used to say: do not be like servants who serve the master in the expectation of receiving a reward, but be like servants who serve the master without the expectation of receiving a reward, and let the fear of Heaven be upon you:

Mishnah 4

Yose ben Yoezer (a man) of Zeredah and Yose ben Yohanan [a man] of Jerusalem received [the oral tradition] from them [i.e. Shimon the Righteous and Antigonus]. Yose ben Yoezer used to say: let thy house be a house of meeting for the Sages and sit in the very dust of their feet, and drink in their words with thirst:

Mishnah 5

Yose ben Yochanan (a man) of Jerusalem used to say: Let thy house be wide open, and let the poor be members of thy household. Engage not in too much conversation with women. They said this with regard to one's own wife, how much more [does the rule apply] with regard to another man's wife. From here the Sages said: as long as a man engages in too much conversation with women, he causes evil to himself, he neglects the study of the Torah, and in the end he will inherit gehinnom:

Mishnah 6

Joshua ben Perahiah and Nittai the Arbelite received [the oral tradition] from them. Joshua ben Perahiah used to say: appoint for thyself a teacher, and acquire for thyself a companion and judge all men with the scale weighted in his favor:

Mishnah 7

Nittai the Arbelite used to say: keep a distance from an evil neighbor, do not become attached to the wicked, and do not abandon faith in [divine] retribution:

Mishnah 8

Judah ben Tabbai and Shimon ben Shetach received [the oral tradition] from them. Judah ben Tabbai said: do not [as a judge] play the part of an advocate; and when the litigants are standing before you, look upon them as if they were [both] guilty; and when they leave your presence, look upon them as if they were [both] innocent, when they have accepted the judgement:

Mishnah 9

Shimon ben Shetach used to say: be thorough in the interrogation of witnesses, and be careful with your words, lest from them they learn to lie:

Mishnah 10

Shemaiah and Abtalion received [the oral tradition] from them. Shemaiah used to say: love work, hate acting the superior, and do not attempt to draw near to the ruling authority:

Mishnah 11

Abtalion used to say: Sages be careful with your words, lest you incur the penalty of exile, and be carried off to a place of evil waters, and the disciples who follow you drink and die, and thus the name of heaven becomes profaned:

Mishnah 12

Hillel and Shammai received [the oral tradition] from them. Hillel used to say: be of the disciples of Aaron, loving peace and pursuing peace, loving mankind and drawing them close to the Torah:

Mishnah 13

He [also] used to say: one who makes his name great causes his name to be destroyed; one who does not add [to his knowledge] causes [it] to cease; one who does not study [the Torah] deserves death; one who makes [unworthy] use of the crown [of learning] shall pass away:

Mishnah 14

He [also] used to say: If I am not for myself, who is for me? But if I am for my own self [only], what am I? And if not now, when?:

Mishnah 15

Shammai used to say: make your [study of the] Torah a fixed practice; speak little, but do much; and receive all men with a pleasant countenance:

Mishnah 16

Rabban Gamaliel used to say: appoint for thyself a teacher, avoid doubt, and do not make a habit of tithing by guesswork.

Mishnah 17

Shimon, his son, used to say: all my days I grew up among the sages, and I have found nothing better for a person than silence. Study is not the most important thing, but actions; whoever indulges in too many words brings about sin:

Mishnah 18

Rabban Shimon ben Gamaliel used to say: on three things does the world stand: On justice, on truth and on peace, as it is said: "execute the judgment of truth and peace in your gates" (Zechariah 8:16).

PIRKEI Chapter 1 AVOT

Chapter 2

Mishnah 1

Rabbi Said: which is the straight path that a man should choose for himself? One which is an honor to the person adopting it, and [on account of which] honor [accrues] to him from others. And be careful with a light commandment as with a grave one, for you did know not the reward for the fulfillment of the commandments. Also, reckon the loss [that may be sustained through the fulfillment] of a commandment against the reward [accruing] thereby, and the gain [that may be obtained through the committing] of a transgression against the loss [entailed] thereby. Apply your mind to three things and you will not come into the clutches of sin: Know what there is above you: An eye that sees, an ear that hears, and all your deeds are written in a book:

Mishnah 2

Rabban Gamaliel the son of Rabbi Judah Hanasi said: excellent is the study of the Torah when combined with a worldly occupation, for toil in them both keeps sin out of one's mind; But [study of the] Torah which is not combined with a worldly occupation, in the end comes to be neglected and becomes the cause of sin. And all who labor with the community, should labor with them for the sake Heaven, for the merit of their forefathers sustains them (the community), and their (the forefather's) righteousness endures for ever; And as for you, [God in such case says] I credit you with a rich reward, as if you [yourselves] had [actually] accomplished [it all]:

Mishnah 3

Be careful [in your dealings] with the ruling authorities for they do not befriend a person except for their own needs; they seem like friends when it is to their own interest, but they do not stand by a man in the hour of his distress:

Mishnah 4

He used to say: do His will as though it were your will, so that He will do your will as though it were His. Set aside your will in the face of His will, so that he may set aside the will of others for the sake of your will. Hillel said: do not separate yourself from the community. Do not trust in yourself until the day of your death. Do not judge not your fellow man until you have reached his place. Do not say something that cannot be understood [trusting] that in the end it will be understood. Say not: 'when I shall have leisure I shall study;' perhaps you will not have leisure:

Mishnah 5

He used to say: A brute is not sin-fearing, nor is an ignorant person pious; nor can a timid person learn, nor can an impatient person teach; nor will someone who engages too much in business become wise. In a place where there are no men, strive to be a man:

Mishnah 6

Moreover, he saw a skull floating on the face of the water. He said to it: because you drowned others, they drowned you. And in the end, they that drowned you will be drowned:

Mishnah 7

He used to say: The more flesh, the more worms; The more property, the more anxiety; The more wives, the more witchcraft; The more female slaves, the more lewdness; The more slaves, the more robbery; [But] the more Torah, the more life; The more sitting [in the company of scholars], the more wisdom; The more counsel, the more understanding; The more charity, the more peace.

If one acquires a good name, he has acquired something for himself; If one acquires for himself knowledge of Torah, he has acquired life in the world to come:

Mishnah 8

Rabban Yohanan ben Zakkai received [the oral tradition] from Hillel and Shammai. He used to say: if you have learned much Torah, do not claim credit for yourself, because for such a purpose were you created. Rabban Yohanan ben Zakkai had five disciples and they were these: Rabbi Eliezer ben Hyrcanus, Rabbi Joshua ben Hananiah, Rabbi Yose, the priest, Rabbi Shimon ben Nethaneel and Rabbi Eleazar ben Arach. He [Rabbi Johanan] used to list their outstanding virtues: Rabbi Eliezer ben Hyrcanus is a plastered cistern which loses not a drop; Rabbi Joshua ben Hananiah happy is the woman that gave birth to him; Rabbi Yose, the priest, is a pious man; Rabbi Simeon ben Nethaneel is one that fears sin, And Rabbi Eleazar ben Arach is like a spring that [ever] gathers force. He [Rabbi Yohanan] used to say: if all the sages of Israel were on one scale of the balance and Rabbi Eliezer ben Hyrcanus on the other scale, he would outweigh them all. Abba Shaul said in his name: if all the sages of Israel were on one scale of the balance, and Rabbi

Eliezer ben Hyrcanus also with them, and Rabbi Eleazar ben Arach on the other scale, he would outweigh them all:

Mishnah 9

He [Rabban Yohanan] said unto them: go forth and observe which is the right way to which a man should cleave? Rabbi Eliezer said, a good eye; Rabbi Joshua said, a good companion; Rabbi Yose said, a good neighbor; Rabbi Shimon said, foresight. Rabbi Elazar said, a good heart. He [Rabban Yohanan] said to them: I prefer the words of Elazar ben Arach, for in his words your words are included. He [Rabban Yohanan] said unto them: go forth and observe which is the evil way which a man should shun? Rabbi Eliezer said, an evil eye; Rabbi Joshua said, an evil companion; Rabbi Yose said, an evil neighbor; Rabbi Shimon said, one who borrows and does not repay for he that borrows from man is as one who borrows from God, blessed be He, as it is said, "the wicked borrow and do not repay, but the righteous deal graciously and give" (Psalms 37:21). Rabbi Elazar said, an evil heart. He [Rabban Yohanan] said to them: I prefer the words of Elazar ben Arach, for in his words your words are included:

Mishnah 10

They [each] said three things: Rabbi Eliezer said: Let the honor of your friend be as dear to you as your own; And be not easily provoked to anger; And repent one day before your death. And [he also said:] warm yourself before the fire of the wise, but beware of being singed by their glowing coals, for their bite is the bite of a fox, and their sting is the sting of a scorpion, and their hiss is the hiss of a serpent, and all their words are like coals of fire:

Mishnah 11

Rabbi Joshua said: an evil eye, the evil inclination, and hatred for humankind put a person out of the world:

Mishnah 12

Rabbi Yose said: Let the property of your fellow be as precious unto you as your own; Make yourself fit to study Torah for it will not be yours by inheritance; And let all your actions be for [the sake of] the name of heaven:

Mishnah 13

Rabbi Shimon said: Be careful with the reading of Shema and the prayer, And when you pray, do not make your prayer something automatic, but a plea for compassion before God, for it is said: "for he is gracious and compassionate, slow to anger, abounding in kindness, and renouncing punishment" (Joel 2:13); And be not wicked in your own esteem:

Mishnah 14

Rabbi Elazar said: Be diligent in the study the Torah; And know how to answer an epicuros, And know before whom you toil, and that your employer is faithful, for He will pay you the reward of your labor:

Mishnah 15

Rabbi Tarfon said: the day is short, and the work is plentiful, and the laborers are indolent, and the reward is great, and the master of the house is insistent:

Mishnah 16

He [Rabbi Tarfon] used to say: It is not your duty to finish the work, but neither are you at liberty to neglect it; If you have studied much Torah, you shall be given much reward. Faithful is your employer to pay you the reward of your labor; And know that the grant of reward unto the righteous is in the age to come.

Chapter 3

Mishnah 1

Akabyah ben Mahalalel said: mark well three things and you will not come into the power of sin: Know from where you come, and where you are going, and before whom you are destined to give an account and reckoning. From where do you come? From a putrid drop. Where are you going? To a place of dust, of worm and of maggot. Before whom you are destined to give an account and reckoning? Before the King of the kings of kings, the Holy One, blessed be he:

Mishnah 2

Rabbi Hanina, the vice-high priest said: pray for the welfare of the government, for were it not for the fear it inspires, every man would swallow his neighbor alive. R. Hananiah ben Teradion said: if two sit together and there are no words of Torah [spoken] between them, then this is a session of scorners, as it is said: "nor sat he in the seat of the scornful…[rather, the teaching of the Lord is his delight]" (Psalms 1:1); but if two sit together and there are words of Torah [spoken] between them, then the Shekhinah abides among them, as it is said: "then they that feared the Lord spoke one with another; and the Lord hearkened and heard, and a book of remembrance was written before Him, for them that feared the Lord and that thought upon His name" (Malachi 3:16). Now I have no [scriptural proof for the presence of the Shekhinah] except [among] two, how [do we know] that even one who sits and studies Torah the Holy One, blessed be He, fixes his reward? As it is said: "though he sit alone and [meditate] in stillness, yet he takes [a reward] unto himself" (Lamentations 3:28):

Mishnah 3

Rabbi Shimon said: if three have eaten at one table and have not spoken there words of Torah, [it is] as if they had eaten sacrifices [offered] to the dead, as it is said, "for all tables are full of filthy vomit, when the All-Present is absent" (Isaiah 28:8). But, if three have eaten at one table, and have spoken there words of Torah, [it is] as if they had eaten at the table of the All-Present, blessed be He, as it is said, "And He said unto me, 'this is the table before the Lord''': (Ezekiel 41:2):

Mishnah 4

Rabbi Hananiah ben Hakinai said: one who wakes

up at night, or walks on the way alone and turns his heart to idle matters, behold, this man is mortally guilty:

Mishnah 5

Rabbi Nehunia ben Hakkanah said: whoever takes upon himself the yoke of the Torah, they remove from him the yoke of government and the yoke of worldly concerns, and whoever breaks off from himself the yoke of the Torah, they place upon him the yoke of government and the yoke of worldly concerns:

Mishnah 6

Rabbi Halafta of Kefar Hanania said: when ten sit together and occupy themselves with Torah, the Shechinah abides among them, as it is said: "God stands in the congregation of God" (Psalm 82:). How do we know that the same is true even of five? As it is said: "This band of His He has established on earth" (Amos 9:6). How do we know that the same is true even of three? As it is said: "In the midst of the judges He judges" (Psalm 82:1) How do we know that the same is true even of two? As it is said: "Then they that fear the Lord spoke one with another, and the Lord hearkened, and heard" (Malachi 3:16). How do we know that the same is true even of one? As it is said: "In every place where I cause my name to be mentioned I will come unto you and bless you" (Exodus 20:21):

Mishnah 7

Rabbi Elazar of Bartotha said: give to Him of that which is His, for you and that which is yours is His; and thus it says with regards to David: "for everything comes from You, and from Your own hand have we given you" (I Chronicles 29:14). Rabbi Jacob said: if one is studying while walking on the road and interrupts his study and says, "how fine is this tree!" [or] "how fine is this newly ploughed field!" scripture accounts it to him as if he was mortally guilty:

Mishnah 8

Rabbi Dostai ben Rabbi Yannai said in the name of Rabbi Meir: whoever forgets one word of his study, scripture accounts it to him as if he were mortally guilty, as it is said, "But take utmost care and watch yourselves scrupulously, so that you do not forget the things that you saw with your own eyes" (Deuteronomy 4:9). One could [have inferred that this is the case] even when his study proved [too] hard for him, therefore scripture says, "that they do not fade from your mind as long as you live" (ibid.). Thus, he is not mortally guilty unless he deliberately removes them from his heart:

Mishnah 9

Rabbi Hanina ben Dosa said: anyone whose fear of sin precedes his wisdom, his wisdom is enduring, but anyone whose wisdom precedes his fear of sin, his wisdom is not enduring. He [also] used to say: anyone whose deeds exceed his wisdom, his wisdom is enduring, but anyone whose wisdom exceeds his deeds, his wisdom is not enduring:

Mishnah 10

He used to say: one with whom men are pleased, God is pleased. But anyone from whom men are displeased, God is displeased. Rabbi Dosa ben Harkinas said: morning sleep, midday wine, children's talk and sitting in the assemblies of the ignorant put a man out of the world:

Mishnah 11

Rabbi Elazar of Modiin said: one who profanes sacred things, and one who despises the festivals, and one who causes his fellow's face to blush in public, and one who annuls the covenant of our father Abraham, may he rest in peace, and he who is contemptuous towards the Torah, even though he has to his credit [knowledge of the] Torah and good deeds, he has not a share in the world to come:

Mishnah 12

Rabbi Ishmael said: be suppliant to a superior, submissive under compulsory service, and receive every man happily:

Mishnah 13

Rabbi Akiva said: Merriment and frivolity accustom one to sexual licentiousness; Tradition is a fence to the Torah; Tithes a fence to wealth, Vows a fence to abstinence; A fence to wisdom is silence:

Mishnah 14

He used to say: Beloved is man for he was created in the image [of God]. Especially beloved is he for it was made known to him that he had been created in the image [of God], as it is said: "for in the image of God He made man" (Genesis 9:6). Beloved are Israel in that they were called children to the All-Present. Especially beloved are they for it was made known to them that they are called children of the All-Present, as it is said: "your are children to the Lord your God" (Deuteronomy 14:1). Beloved are Israel in that a precious vessel was given to them. Especially beloved are they for it was made known to them that the desirable instrument, with which the world had been created, was given to them, as it is said: "for I give you good instruction; forsake not my teaching" (Proverbs 4:2):

Mishnah 15

Everything is foreseen yet freedom of choice is granted, And the world is judged with goodness; And everything is in accordance with the preponderance of works:

Mishnah 16

He used to say: everything is given against a pledge, and a net is spread out over all the living; the store is open and the storekeeper allows credit, but the ledger is open and the hand writes, and whoever wishes to borrow may come and borrow; but the collectors go round regularly every day and exact dues from man, either with his consent or without his consent, and they have that on which they [can] rely [in their claims], seeing that the judgment is a righteous judgment, and everything is prepared for the banquet:

Mishnah 7

Rabbi Elazar ben Azariah says: If there is no Torah, there is no worldly occupation, if there is no worldly occupation, there is no Torah. If there is no wisdom, there is no fear of God; if there is no fear of God, there is no wisdom. If there is no knowledge, there is no understanding; if there is no understanding, there is no knowledge. If there is no flour, there is no Torah; if there is no Torah, there is no flour. He used to say: Anyone whose wisdom exceeds his deeds, to what is he compared? To a tree who branches are many but whose roots are few; then the winds comes and uproots it and turns it upside down; as it is said; "And he shall be like a lonely juniper tree in the wasteland and shall not see when good comes, but shall inhabit the parched places of the wilderness, a salt filled land which is uninhabitable." [Jeremiah 17:6]. But one whose deeds exceed one's wisdom, what is that person like? Like a tree whose branches are few, but whose roots are many; even if all the winds of the world were to come and blow upon it, they would not move it from its place, as it is said; "He shall be like a tree planted by the waters, which spreads out its roots by the river, and shall not perceive when heat comes, but its leaf shall remain fresh; and it will not be troubled in the year of drought, nor will it cease to bear fruit." [Jeremiah 17:8]:

Mishnah 18

Rabbi Eliezer Hisma said: the laws of mixed bird offerings and the key to the calculations of menstruation days these, these are the body of the halakhah. The calculation of the equinoxes and gematria are the desserts of wisdom:

PIRKEI Chapter 3 AVOT

Chapter 4

Mishnah 1

Ben Zoma said: Who is wise? He who learns from every man, as it is said: "From all who taught me have I gained understanding" (Psalms 119:99). Who is mighty? He who subdues his [evil] inclination, as it is said: "He that is slow to anger is better than the mighty; and he that rules his spirit than he that takes a city" (Proverbs 16:3). Who is rich? He who rejoices in his lot, as it is said: "You shall enjoy the fruit of your labors, you shall be happy and you shall prosper" (Psalms 128:2) "You shall be happy" in this world, "and you shall prosper" in the world to come. Who is he that is honored? He who honors his fellow human beings as it is said: "For I honor those that honor Me, but those who spurn Me shall be dishonored" (I Samuel 2:30):

Mishnah 2

Ben Azzai said: Be quick in performing a minor commandment as in the case of a major one, and flee from transgression; For one commandment leads to another commandment, and transgression leads to another transgression; For the reward for performing a commandment is another commandment and the reward for committing a transgression is a transgression:

Mishnah 3

He used to say: do not despise any man, and do not discriminate against anything, for there is no man that has not his hour, and there is no thing that has not its place:

Mishnah 4

Rabbi Levitas a man of Yavneh said: be exceeding humble spirit, for the end of man is the worm. Rabbi Yohanan ben Berokah said: whoever profanes the name of heaven in secret, he shall be punished in the open. Unwittingly or wittingly, it is all one in profaning the name:

Mishnah 5

Rabbi Ishmael his son said: He who learns in order to teach, it is granted to him to study and to teach; But he who learns in order to practice, it is granted to him to learn and to teach and to practice. Rabbi Zadok said: do not make them a crown for self-exaltation, nor a spade with which to dig. So too Hillel used to say, "And he that puts the crown to his own use shall perish". Thus, you have learned, anyone who derives worldly benefit from the words of the Torah, removes his life from the world:

Mishnah 6

Rabbi Yose said: whoever honors the Torah is himself honored by others, and whoever dishonors the Torah is himself dishonored by others:

Mishnah 7

Rabbi Ishmael his son said: he who refrains himself from judgment, rids himself of enmity, robbery and false swearing; But he whose heart is presumptuous in giving a judicial decision, is foolish, wicked and arrogant:

Mishnah 8

He used to say: judge not alone, for none may judge alone save one. And say not "accept my view", for they are free but not you:

Mishnah 9

Rabbi Jonathan said: whoever fulfills the Torah out of a state of poverty, his end will be to fulfill it out of a state of wealth; And whoever discards.

The Torah out of a state of wealth, his end will be to discard it out of a state of poverty:

Mishnah 10

Rabbi Meir said: Engage but little in business, and busy yourself with the Torah. Be of humble spirit before all men. If you have neglected the Torah, you shall have many who bring you to neglect it, but if you have labored at the study of Torah, there is much reward to give unto you:

Mishnah 11

Rabbi Eliezer son of Yaakov says: One who does a single good deed acquires a single defender. One who does a single sin acquires a single prosecutor. Repentance and good deeds are a shield against punishment. Rabbi Yochanan the shoemaker said: Every gathering that is for the sake of Heaven will endure. And every gathering that isn't for the sake of Heaven will not endure, in the end:

Mishnah 12

Rabbi Elazar ben Shammua said: let the honor of your student be as dear to you as your own, and the honor of your colleague as the reverence for your teacher, and the reverence for your teacher as the reverence of heaven:

Mishnah 13

Rabbi Judah said: be careful in study, for an error in study counts as deliberate sin. Rabbi Shimon said: There are three crowns: the crown of torah, the crown of priesthood, and the crown of royalty, but the crown of a good name supersedes them all:

Mishnah 14

Rabbi Nehorai said: go as a [voluntary] exile to a place of Torah and say not that it will come after you, for [it is] your fellow [student]s who will make it permanent in your hand and "and lean not upon your own understanding" (Proverbs 3:5):

Mishnah 15

Rabbi Yannai said: it is not in our hands [to explain the reason] either of the security of the wicked, or even of the afflictions of the righteous. Rabbi Mathia ben Harash said: Upon meeting people, be the first to extend greetings; And be a tail unto lions, and not a head unto foxes:

Mishnah 16

Rabbi Jacob said: this world is like a vestibule before the world to come; prepare yourself in the vestibule, so that you may enter the banqueting-hall:

Mishnah 17

He used to say: more precious is one hour in repentance and good deeds in this world, than all the life of the world to come; And more precious is one hour of the tranquility of the world to come, than all the life of this world:

Mishnah 18

Rabbi Shimon ben Elazar said: Do not try to appease your friend during his hour of anger; Nor comfort him at the hour while his dead still lies before him; Nor question him at the hour of his vow; Nor strive to see him in the hour of his disgrace:

Mishnah 19

Shmuel Hakatan said: "If your enemy falls, do not exult; if he trips, let your heart not rejoice, lest the Lord see it and be displeased, and avert his wrath from him" (Proverbs 24:17):

Mishnah 20

Elisha ben Abuyah said: He who learns when a

child, to what is he compared? To ink written upon a new writing sheet. And he who learns when an old man, to what is he compared? To ink written on a rubbed writing sheet. Rabbi Yose ben Judah a man of Kfar Ha-babli said: He who learns from the young, to what is he compared? To one who eats unripe grapes, and drinks wine from his vat; And he who learns from the old, to what is he compared? To one who eats ripe grapes, and drinks old wine. Rabbi said: don't look at the container but at that which is in it: there is a new container full of old wine, and an old [container] in which there is not even new [wine]:

Mishnah 21

Rabbi Elazar Ha-kappar said: envy, lust and [the desire for] honor put a man out of the world:

Mishnah 22

He used to say: the ones who were born are to die, and the ones who have died are to be brought to life, and the ones brought to life are to be judged; So that one may know, make known and have the knowledge that He is God, He is the designer, He is the creator, He is the discerner, He is the judge, He the witness, He the complainant, and that He will summon to judgment. Blessed be He, before Whom there is no iniquity, nor forgetting, nor respect of persons, nor taking of bribes, for all is His. And know that all is according to the reckoning. And let not your impulse assure thee that the grave is a place of refuge for you; for against your will were you formed, against your will were you born, against your will you live, against your will you will die, and against your will you will give an account and reckoning before the King of the kings of kings, the Holy One, blessed be He:

Chapter 5

Mishnah 1

With ten utterances the world was created. And what does this teach, for surely it could have been created with one utterance? But this was so in order to punish the wicked who destroy the world that was created with ten utterances, and to give a good reward to the righteous who maintain the world that was created with ten utterances:

Mishnah 2

[There were] ten generations from Adam to Noah, in order to make known what long-suffering is His; for all those generations kept on provoking Him, until He brought upon them the waters of the flood. [There were] ten generations from Noah to Abraham, in order to make known what long-suffering is His; for all those generations kept on provoking Him, until Abraham, came and received the reward of all of them:

Mishnah 3

With ten trials was Abraham, our father (may he rest in peace), tried, and he withstood them all; to make known how great was the love of Abraham, our father (peace be upon him):

Mishnah 4

Ten miracles were wrought for our ancestors in Egypt, and ten at the sea. Ten plagues did the Holy one, blessed be He, bring upon the Egyptians in Egypt and ten at the sea. [With] ten trials did our ancestors try God, blessed be He, as it is said, "and they have tried Me these ten times and they have not listened to my voice" (Numbers 14:22):

Mishnah 5

Ten wonders were wrought for our ancestors in the Temple:
[1] no woman miscarried from the odor of the sacred flesh;
[2] the sacred flesh never became putrid;
[3] no fly was ever seen in the slaughterhouse;
[4] no emission occurred to the high priest on the Day of Atonement;
[5] the rains did not extinguish the fire of the woodpile;
[6] the wind did not prevail against the column of smoke;
[7] no defect was found in the omer, or in the two loaves, or in the showbread;

[8] the people stood pressed together, yet bowed down and had room enough;
[9] never did a serpent or a scorpion harm anyone in Jerusalem;
[10] and no man said to his fellow: the place is too congested for me to lodge overnight in Jerusalem:

Mishnah 6

Ten things were created on the eve of the Sabbath at twilight, and these are they:
[1] the mouth of the earth,
[2] the mouth of the well,
[3] the mouth of the donkey,
[4] the rainbow,
[5] the manna,
[6] the staff [of Moses],
[7] the shamir,
[8] the letters,
[9] the writing,
[10] and the tablets.
And some say: also, the demons, the grave of Moses, and the ram of Abraham, our father. And some say: and also, tongs, made with tongs:

Mishnah 7

[There are] seven things [characteristic] in a clod, and seven in a wise man: A wise man does not speak before one who is greater than he in wisdom, And does not break into his fellow's speech; And is not hasty to answer; He asks what is relevant, and he answers to the point; And he speaks of the first [point] first, and of the last [point] last; And concerning that which he has not heard, he says: I have not heard; And he acknowledges the truth. And the reverse of these [are characteristic] in a clod:

Mishnah 8

Seven kinds of punishment come to the world for seven categories of transgression: When some of them give tithes, and others do not give tithes, a famine from drought comes some go hungry, and others are satisfied. When they have all decided not to give tithes, a famine from tumult and drought comes; [When they have, in addition, decided] not to set apart the dough-offering, an all-consuming famine comes. Pestilence comes to the world for sins punishable by death according to the Torah, but which have not been referred to the court, and for neglect of the law regarding the fruits of the sabbatical year. The sword comes to the world for the delay of judgment, and for the perversion of judgment, and because of those who teach the Torah not in accordance with the accepted law:

Mishnah 9

Wild beasts come to the world for swearing in vain, and for the profanation of the Name. Exile comes to the world for idolatry, for sexual sins and for bloodshed, and for [transgressing the commandment of] the [year of the] release of the land. At four times pestilence increases: in the fourth year, in the seventh year and at the conclusion of the seventh year, and at the conclusion of the Feast [of Tabernacles] in every year. In the fourth year, on account of the tithe of the poor which is due in the third year. In the seventh year, on account of the tithe of the poor which is due in the sixth year; At the conclusion of the seventh year, on account of the produce of the seventh year; And at the conclusion of the Feast [of Tabernacles] in every year, for robbing the gifts to the poor:

Mishnah 10

There are four types of character in human beings: One that says: "mine is mine, and yours is yours": this is a commonplace type; and some say this is a sodom-type of character. [One that says:] "mine is yours and yours is mine": is an unlearned person (am haaretz); [One that says:] "mine is yours and yours is yours" is a pious person. [One that says:]

"mine is mine, and yours is mine" is a wicked person:

Mishnah 11

There are four kinds of temperaments: Easy to become angry, and easy to be appeased: his gain disappears in his loss; Hard to become angry, and hard to be appeased: his loss disappears in his gain; Hard to become angry and easy to be appeased: a pious person; Easy to become angry and hard to be appeased: a wicked person:

Mishnah 12

There are four types of disciples: Quick to comprehend, and quick to forget: his gain disappears in his loss; Slow to comprehend, and slow to forget: his loss disappears in his gain; Quick to comprehend, and slow to forget: he is a wise man; Slow to comprehend, and quick to forget, this is an evil portion:

Mishnah 13

There are four types of charity givers. He who wishes to give, but that others should not give: his eye is evil to that which belongs to others; He who wishes that others should give, but that he himself should not give: his eye is evil towards that which is his own; He who desires that he himself should give, and that others should give: he is a pious man; He who desires that he himself should not give and that others too should not give: he is a wicked man:

Mishnah 14

There are four types among those who frequent the study-house (bet midrash): He who attends but does not practice: he receives a reward for attendance. He who practices but does not attend: he receives a reward for practice. He who attends and practices: he is a pious man; He who neither attends nor practices: he is a wicked man:

Mishnah 15

There are four types among those who sit before the sages: a sponge, a funnel, a strainer and a sieve. A sponge, soaks up everything; A funnel, takes in at one end and lets out at the other; A strainer, which lets out the wine and retains the lees; A sieve, which lets out the coarse meal and retains the choice flour:

Mishnah 16

All love that depends on a something, [when the] thing ceases, [the] love ceases; and [all love] that does not depend on anything, will never cease. What is an example of love that depended on a something? Such was the love of Amnon for Tamar. And what is an example of love that did not depend on anything? Such was the love of David and Jonathan:

Mishnah 17

Every dispute that is for the sake of Heaven, will in the end endure; But one that is not for the sake of Heaven, will not endure. Which is the controversy that is for the sake of Heaven? Such was the controversy of Hillel and Shammai. And which is the controversy that is not for the sake of Heaven? Such was the controversy of Korah and all his congregation:

Mishnah 18

Whoever causes the multitudes to be righteous, sin will not occur on his account; And whoever causes the multitudes to sin, they do not give him the ability to repent. Moses was righteous and caused the multitudes to be righteous, [therefore] the righteousness of the multitudes is hung on him, as it is said, "He executed the Lord's righteousness and His decisions with Israel" (Deut. 33:21). Jeroboam, sinned and caused the multitudes to sin, [therefore] the sin of the multitudes is hung on him, as it is said, "For the sins of Jeroboam which he sinned, and which he caused Israel to sin thereby" (I Kings 15:30):

Mishnah 19

Whoever possesses these three things, he is of the disciples of Abraham, our father; and [whoever possesses] three other things, he is of the disciples of Balaam, the wicked. A good eye, a humble spirit and a moderate appetite he is of the disciples of Abraham, our father. An evil eye, a haughty spirit and a limitless appetite he is of the disciples of Balaam, the wicked. What is the difference between the disciples of Abraham, our father, and the disciples of Balaam, the wicked? The disciples of Abraham, our father, enjoy this world, and inherit the world to come, as it is said: "I will endow those who love me with substance, I will fill their treasuries" (Proverbs 8:21). But the disciples of Balaam, the wicked, inherit gehinnom, and descend into the nethermost pit, as it is said: "For you, O God, will bring them down to the nethermost pit those murderous and treacherous men; they shall not live out half their days; but I trust in You" (Psalms 55:24):

Mishnah 20

Judah ben Tema said: Be strong as a leopard, and swift as an eagle, and fleet as a gazelle, and brave as a lion, to do the will of your Father who is in heaven. He used to say: the arrogant is headed for Gehinnom and the blushing for the garden of Eden. May it be the will, O Lord our God, that your city be rebuilt speedily in our days and set our portion in the studying of your Torah:

Mishnah 21

He used to say: At five years of age the study of Scripture; At ten the study of Mishnah; At thirteen subject to the commandments; At fifteen the study of Talmud; At eighteen the bridal canopy; At twenty for pursuit [of livelihood]; At thirty the peak of strength; At forty wisdom; At fifty able to give counsel; At sixty old age; At seventy fullness of years; At eighty the age of "strength"; At ninety a bent body; At one hundred, as good as dead and gone completely out of the world:

Mishnah 22

Ben Bag Bag said: Turn it over, and [again] turn it over, for all is therein. And look into it; And become gray and old therein; And do not move away from it, for you have no better portion than it.

Mishnah 23

Ben He He said: According to the labor is the reward.

PIRKEI   Chapter 5   AVOT

Chapter 6

Mishnah 1

The sages taught in the language of the mishnah. Blessed be He who chose them and their teaching. Rabbi Meir said: Whoever occupies himself with the Torah for its own sake, merits many things; not only that but he is worth the whole world. He is called beloved friend; one that loves God; one that loves humankind; one that gladdens God; one that gladdens humankind. And the Torah clothes him in humility and reverence, and equips him to be righteous, pious, upright and trustworthy; it keeps him far from sin, and brings him near to merit. And people benefit from his counsel, sound knowledge, understanding and strength, as it is said, "Counsel is mine and sound wisdom; I am understanding, strength is mine" (Proverbs 8:14). And it bestows upon him royalty, dominion, and acuteness in judgment. To him are revealed the secrets of the Torah, and he is made as an ever-flowing spring, and like a stream that never ceases. And he becomes modest, long-suffering and forgiving of insult. And it magnifies him and exalts him over everything:

Mishnah 2

Rabbi Joshua ben Levi said: every day a bat kol (a heavenly voice) goes forth from Mount Horeb and makes proclamation and says: "Woe unto humankind for their contempt towards the Torah", for whoever does not occupy himself with the study of Torah is called, nazuf (the rebuked. As it is said, "Like a gold ring in the snout of a pig is a beautiful woman bereft of sense" (Proverbs 22:11). And it says, "And the tablets were the work of God, and the writing was the writing of God, graven upon the tablets" (Exodus 32:16). Read not haruth ['graven'] but heruth ['freedom']. For there is no free man but one that occupies himself with the study of the Torah. And whoever regularly occupies himself with the study of the Torah he is surely exalted, as it is said, "And from Mattanah to Nahaliel; and Nahaliel to Bamoth" (Numbers 21:19):

Mishnah 3

One who learns from his fellow one chapter, or one halakhah, or one verse, or one word, or even one letter, is obligated to treat him with honor; for so we find with David, king of Israel, who learned from Ahitophel no more than two things, yet called him his master, his guide and his beloved friend, as it is said, "But it was you, a man mine equal, my guide and my beloved friend" (Psalms 55:14). Is this not [an instance of the argument] "from the less to the greater" (kal vehomer)? If David, king of Israel who learned from Ahitophel no more than two things, nevertheless called him his master, his guide and his beloved friend; then in the case of one who learns from his fellow one chapter, or one halakhah, or one verse, or one word, or even one letter, all the more so he is under obligation to treat him with honor. And "honor"' means nothing but Torah, as it is said, "It is honor that sages inherit" (Proverbs 3:35). "And the perfect shall inherit good" (Proverbs 28:10), and "good" means nothing but Torah, as it is said, "For I give you good instruction; do not forsake my Torah" (Proverbs 4:2):

Mishnah 4

Such is the way [of a life] of Torah: you shall eat bread with salt, and rationed water shall you drink; you shall sleep on the ground, your life will be one of privation, and in Torah shall you labor. If you do this, "Happy shall you be and it shall be good for you" (Psalms 128:2): "Happy shall you be" in this world, "and it shall be good for you" in the world to come.

PIRKEI AVOT
Chapter 6

Mishnah 5

Do not seek greatness for yourself, and do not covet honor. Practice more than you learn. Do not yearn for the table of kings, for your table is greater than their table, and your crown is greater than their crown, and faithful is your employer to pay you the reward of your labor:

Mishnah 6

Greater is learning Torah than the priesthood and than royalty, for royalty is acquired by thirty stages, and the priesthood by twenty-four, but the Torah by forty-eight things. By study, Attentive listening, Proper speech, By an understanding heart, By an intelligent heart, By awe, By fear, By humility, By joy, By attending to the sages, By critical give and take with friends, By fine argumentation with disciples, By clear thinking, By study of Scripture, By study of mishnah, By a minimum of sleep, By a minimum of chatter, By a minimum of pleasure, By a minimum of frivolity, By a minimum of preoccupation with worldly matters, By long-suffering, By generosity, By faith in the sages, By acceptance of suffering. [Learning of Torah is also acquired by one] Who recognizes his place, Who rejoices in his portion, Who makes a fence about his words,

Who takes no credit for himself, Who is loved, Who loves God, Who loves [his fellow] creatures, Who loves righteous ways, Who loves reproof, Who loves uprightness, Who keeps himself far from honors, Who does not let his heart become swelled on account of his learning, Who does not delight in giving legal decisions, Who shares in the bearing of a burden with his colleague, Who judges with the scales weighted in his favor, Who leads him on to truth, Who leads him on to peace, Who composes himself at his study, Who asks and answers, Who listens [to others], and [himself] adds [to his knowledge], Who learns in order to teach, Who learns in order to practice, Who makes his teacher wiser, Who is exact in what he has learned, And who says a thing in the name of him who said it. Thus, you have learned: everyone who says a thing in the name of him who said it, brings deliverance into the world, as it is said: "And Esther told the king in Mordecai's name" (Esther 2:22):

Mishnah 7

Great is Torah for it gives life to those that practice it, in this world, and in the world to come, As it is said: "For they are life unto those that find them, and health to all their flesh" (Proverbs 4:22), And it says: "It will be a cure for your navel and marrow for your bones" (ibid. 3:8) And it says: "She is a tree of life to those that grasp her, and whoever holds onto her is happy" (ibid. 3:18), And it says: "For they are a graceful wreath upon your head, a necklace about your throat" (ibid. 1:9), And it says: "She will adorn your head with a graceful wreath; crown you with a glorious diadem" (ibid. 4:9) And it says: "In her right hand is length of days, in her left riches and honor" (ibid. 3:1, And it says: "For they will bestow on you length of days, years of life and peace" (ibid. 3:2):

Mishnah 8

Rabbi Shimon ben Menasya said in the name of Rabbi Shimon ben Yohai: Beauty, strength, riches, honor, wisdom, [old age], gray hair, and children are becoming to the righteous, and becoming to the world, As it is said: "Gray hair is a crown of glory (beauty); it is attained by way of righteousness" (Proverbs 16:3, And it says: "The ornament of the wise is their wealth" (ibid. 14:24), And it says: "Grandchildren are the glory of their elders, and the glory of children is their parents" (ibid. 17:6), And it says: "The glory of youths is their strength; and the beauty of old men is their gray hair" (ibid. 20:29), And it says: "Then the moon shall be ashamed, and the sun shall be abashed. For the Lord of Hosts will reign on Mount Zion and in Jerusalem, and God's Honor will be revealed to his elders" (Isaiah 24:23). Rabbi Shimon ben Menasya said: these seven qualities, which the sages have listed [as becoming] to the righteous, were all of them fulfilled in Rabbi and his sons:

Mishnah 9

Rabbi Yose ben Kisma said: Once I was walking by the way when a man met me, and greeted me and I greeted him. He said to me, "Rabbi, where are you from?" I said to him, "I am from a great city of sages and scribes". He said to me, "Rabbi, would you consider living with us in our place? I would give you a thousand thousand denarii of gold, and precious stones and pearls." I said to him: "My son, even if you were to give me all the silver and gold, precious stones and pearls that are in the world, I would not dwell anywhere except in a place of Torah; for when a man passes away there accompany him neither gold nor silver, nor precious stones nor pearls, but Torah and good deeds alone, as it is said, "When you walk it will lead you. When you lie down it will watch over you; and when you are awake it will talk with you" (Proverbs 6:22). "When you walk it will lead you" in this world. "When you lie down it will watch over you" in the grave; "And when you are awake it will talk with you" in the world to come. And thus it is written in the book of Psalms by David, king of Israel, "I prefer the teaching You proclaimed to thousands of pieces of gold and silver" (Psalms 119:71), And it says: "Mine is the silver, and mine the gold, says the Lord of Hosts" (Haggai 2:8):

Mishnah 10

Five possessions did the Holy Blessed One, set aside as his own in this world, and these are they: The Torah, one possession; Heaven and earth, another possession; Abraham, another possession; Israel, another possession; The Temple, another possession:

[1] The Torah is one possession. From where do we know this? Since it is written, "The Lord possessed (usually translated as 'created' me at the beginning of his course, at the first of His works of old" (Proverbs 8:22).

[2] Heaven and earth, another possession. From where do we know this? Since it is said: "Thus said the Lord: The heaven is My throne and the earth is My footstool; Where could you build a house for Me, What place could serve as My abode? (Isaiah 66:1) And it says: "How many are the things You have made, O Lord; You have

made them all with wisdom; the earth is full of Your possessions" (Psalms 104:24).

[3] Abraham is another possession. From where do we know this? Since it is written: "He blessed him, saying, "Blessed by Abram of God Most High, Possessor of heaven and earth" (Genesis 15:19).

[4] Israel is another possession. From where do we know this? Since it is written: "Till Your people cross over, O Lord, Till Your people whom You have possessed" (Exodus 15:16). And it says: "As to the holy and mighty ones that are in the land, my whole desire (possession) is in them" (Psalms 16:3).

[5] The Temple is another possession. From where do we know this? Since it is said: "The sanctuary, O lord, which your hands have established" (Exodus 15:17", And it says: "And He brought them to His holy realm, to the mountain, which His right hand had possessed" (Psalms 78:54).

Mishnah 11

Whatever the Holy Blessed One created in His world, he created only for His glory, as it is said: "All who are linked to My name, whom I have created, formed and made for My glory" (Isaiah 43:7), And it says: "The Lord shall reign for ever and ever" (Exodus 15:18):

Said Rabbi Hananiah ben Akashya: It pleased the Holy Blessed One to grant merit to Israel, that is why He gave them Torah and commandments in abundance, as it is said, "The Lord was pleased for His righteousness, to make Torah great and glorious" (Isaiah 42:21):